Goetia Demons Rope Magick

S ROB

DEDICATION

I dedicate this book to my mother and father.

CONTENTS

Acknowledgments   I

1   Chapter 1   1

2   Chapter 2   Pg 11

3   Chapter 3   Pg 20

4   Chapter 4   Pg 31

5   Chapter 5   Pg 41

6   Chapter 6   Pg 51

7   Chapter 7   Pg 61

8   Chapter 8   Pg 71

ACKNOWLEDGMENTS

I acknowledge the existence of real magick.

Chapter 1

The magick in this book will call upon the power of those demonic beings classified as goetia: these being demons and devils from one particular system of satanism. However, to do so you will need a length of rope long enough to tie several knots in and also it should be easy to untie so you may if you wish halt the magick. This magick here is of a type classified as sympathetic magick and this is when something: in this case rope: represents something so much that acting on it will affect the other thing. In this magick it means quite simply that untying the knots will undo the magick that is done through the rituals within here. In fact, the tying of the knots is a part of the ritual itself and is definitely not some side issue. I do advise that you consider labelling the rope used so you will know what it is for: what ritual it was used in. But within the rituals here you will be summoning one or more demon and to do this you will be using a devil named Leviathan, and Leviathan is often best thought of as a large sea monster type of creature and it is so large that its mouth is in fact the mouth of Hell itself; the Hell Mouth. This means that when we get Leviathan to open its mouth, we are opening the gates of Hell itself. This means we can then summon devils and demon through, tell them what we want of them and get them to leave and get Leviathan to shut its mouth again and the Gates of Hell will have closed.

The first demon you will be summoning is for Baal and he is also the first King of Hell and he is commander of 66 demons. This also means that if required that Baal can pull upon things that seem out of his realm of power when really they are not because as the first King of Hell he may pull on all that is below him: all of the other devils and demons because in this structure Lucifer is more like a god of Hell rather than actually in charge. The first magick you will learn is for greater strength because strength rarely works against us. However, bear in mind that strength as defined by a demon

2

need not be the sort of ugly too large strength many humans desire because to a demon strength that actually gets in the way of fighting is not just no good but counterproductive. No demons and devils have not the need for perfection always and many demons exist that are badly disabled: that is right Hell had the Paralympics first. In fact, many demons and devils are very practical while also be linked to knowledge and creativity as much as any other set of entities I have seen. But to work this magick you will need to go and get a length of rope suitable in length to tie 3 or 4 completely separate knots in it: and to untie them when required.

Protection magick with Baal

(You will need a length of rope long enough to tie several knots in and wide enough in girth for those very same knots to be easy to untie)

Leviathan you are a great monster a powerful devil and your mouth is the very mouth of Hell itself; the Hell Mouth. Leviathan I ask that you open your mouth that which is the gateway of Hell itself; the Gates of Hell. Leviathan open the gates open your mouth: Leviathan opens its mouth the Gates of Hell are open.

TIE THE FIRST KNOT IN THE ROPE

I summon the demonic entity known as Baal through the Gates of Hell. Baal first King of Hell I ask that you step through the gateway and be right here with me: Baal steps through the gates and is here with me.

TIE A SECOND KNOT IN THE ROPE

Baal you are the first King of Hell, he with three heads, one of a toad, one of a man and one of a cat and you have 66 legions of demons at your control. Baal, I ask that you protect me from all harm and this is what I ask of you.

TIE A THIRD KNOT

Baal agrees and departs back through the gates. Leviathan you are a great monster a powerful devil and your mouth is the very mouth of Hell itself; the Hell Mouth. Leviathan I ask that you shut your mouth that which is the gateway of Hell itself; the Gates of Hell. Leviathan close the gates close your mouth: Leviathan closes its mouth the Gates of Hell are shut.

TIE A FOURTH KNOT

So it is and will be.

I feel that as it is unlikely that the person reading this is a monk and they aren't allowed to own possessions then you will have possessions and desire to protect them and so I offer magick to help you do just that. I know that the things we own for most of us become a part of us and never is this truer when they are items we wear. I know that when we lose our watch, spectacles and most of our clothing we do not feel truly ourselves. But it is also true that what makes us unique is what is within us and so do work this potent magick: here it is.

Magick with Baal to protect your possessions

(You will need a length of rope long enough to tie several knots in and wide enough in girth for those very same knots to be easy to untie)

Leviathan you are a great monster a powerful devil and your mouth is the very mouth of Hell itself; the Hell Mouth. Leviathan I ask that you open your mouth that which is the gateway of Hell itself; the Gates of Hell. Leviathan open the gates open your mouth: Leviathan opens its mouth the Gates of Hell are open.

TIE THE FIRST KNOT IN THE ROPE

I summon the demonic entity known as Baal through the Gates of Hell. Baal first King of Hell I ask that you step through the gateway and be right here with me: Baal steps through the gates and is here with me.

TIE A SECOND KNOT IN THE ROPE

Baal you are the first King of Hell, he with three heads, one of a toad, one of a man and one of a cat and you have 66 legions of demons at your control. Baal, I ask that you protect my possessions, all that I own from all harm and from being stolen from me and this is what I ask of you.

TIE A THIRD KNOT

Baal agrees and departs back through the gates. Leviathan you are a great monster a powerful devil and your mouth is the very mouth of Hell itself; the Hell Mouth. Leviathan I ask that you close your mouth that which is the gateway of Hell itself; the Gates of Hell. Leviathan close the gates close your mouth: Leviathan closes its mouth the Gates of Hell are shut.

TIE A FOURTH KNOT

So it is and will be.

Our family is precious to us and so do use this magick and you will see that you can protect your family just that one more level than they are already through the use of magick. There is also one other reason and that is that when things go wrong with family, we probably get dragged into their personal fuck ups: their mistakes and misfortunes. We all know how time consuming this can be so deal with this potential problem through using this magick.

Magick with Baal to protect your family

(You will need a length of rope long enough to tie several knots in and wide enough in girth for those very same knots to be easy to untie)

Leviathan you are a great monster a powerful devil and your mouth is the very mouth of Hell itself; the Hell Mouth. Leviathan I ask

that you open your mouth that which is the gateway of Hell itself; the Gates of Hell. Leviathan open the gates open your mouth: Leviathan opens its mouth the Gates of Hell are open.

TIE THE FIRST KNOT IN THE ROPE

I summon the demonic entity known as Baal through the Gates of Hell. Baal first King of Hell I ask that you step through the gateway and be right here with me: Baal steps through the gates and is here with me.

TIE A SECOND KNOT IN THE ROPE

Baal you are the first King of Hell, he with three heads, one of a toad, one of a man and one of a cat and you have 66 legions of demons at your control. Baal, I ask that you protect all of my family from all attacks and all harm no matter what the source and this is what I ask of you.

TIE A THIRD KNOT

Baal agrees and departs back through the gates. Leviathan you are a great monster a powerful devil and your mouth is the very mouth of Hell itself; the Hell Mouth. Leviathan I ask that you close your mouth that which is the gateway of Hell itself; the Gates of Hell. Leviathan close the gates close your mouth: Leviathan closes its mouth the Gates of Hell are shut.

TIE A FOURTH KNOT

So it is and will be.

You have made a good beginning and so with this in mind I think that we should all use at least some of the magick here. But it is also a good idea to label the rope with some piece of paper tapped on which tells you what the rope is for. I say this because if you ever wish to end its effects then untie the knots. In the reverse of this means that as long as the knots are tied that you have the magick still working.

Chapter 2

To be defeated is not as good as to be victorious however being defeated is often just a short-term fate and all people, male and female, trans and the very old and the very young and all others left can overcome defeat. In fact, this following magick is to help you to become victorious: to have the magick for this fate with you: just keep the knots tied.

Magick with Baal for victory

(You will need a length of rope long enough to tie several knots in and wide enough in girth for those very same knots to be easy to untie)

Leviathan you are a great monster a powerful devil and your mouth is the very mouth of Hell itself; the Hell Mouth. Leviathan I ask that you open your mouth that which is the gateway of Hell itself;

the Gates of Hell. Leviathan open the gates open your mouth: Leviathan opens its mouth the Gates of Hell are open.

TIE THE FIRST KNOT IN THE ROPE

I summon the demonic entity known as Baal through the Gates of Hell. Baal first King of Hell I ask that you step through the gateway and be right here with me: Baal steps through the gates and is here with me.

TIE A SECOND KNOT IN THE ROPE

Baal you are the first King of Hell, he with three heads, one of a toad, one of a man and one of a cat and you have 66 legions of demons at your control. Baal, I ask that you help me be victorious whenever the opportunity presents itself and this is what I ask of you.

TIE A THIRD KNOT

Baal agrees and departs back through the gates. Leviathan you are a great monster a powerful devil and your mouth is the very mouth of Hell itself; the Hell Mouth. Leviathan I ask that you shut your mouth that which is the gateway of Hell itself; the Gates of Hell. Leviathan close the gates close your mouth: Leviathan closes its mouth the Gates of Hell are shut.

TIE A FOURTH KNOT

So it is and will be.

Lots of the time in life it isn't people which cause us the greatest difficulties it is problems. Its easy to think that all problems are man made but to me many seem to be more about bad luck, randomness that anything else. I wish to tackle this using my abilities as an author to teach others what follows. Will what follows to work, keep the knots tied and it will keep working for you.

Magick with Baal to be victorious over problems

(You will need a length of rope long enough to tie several knots in and wide enough in girth for those very same knots to be easy to untie)

Leviathan you are a great monster a powerful devil and your mouth is the very mouth of Hell itself; the Hell Mouth. Leviathan I ask that you open your mouth that which is the gateway of Hell itself; the Gates of Hell. Leviathan open the gates open your mouth: Leviathan opens its mouth the Gates of Hell are open.

TIE THE FIRST KNOT IN THE ROPE

I summon the demonic entity known as Baal through the Gates of Hell. Baal first King of Hell I ask that you step through the gateway and be right here with me: Baal steps through the gates and is here with me.

TIE A SECOND KNOT IN THE ROPE

Baal you are the first King of Hell, he with three heads, one of a toad, one of a man and one of a cat and you have 66 legions of demons at your control. Baal, I ask that you make me victorious over all problems and this is what I ask of you.

TIE A THIRD KNOT

Baal agrees and departs back through the gates. Leviathan you are a great monster a powerful devil and your mouth is the very mouth of Hell itself; the Hell Mouth. Leviathan I ask that you shut your mouth that which is the gateway of Hell itself; the Gates of Hell. Leviathan close the gates close your mouth: Leviathan closes its mouth the Gates of Hell are shut.

TIE A FOURTH KNOT

So it is and will be.

In life there are sometimes problem people: people that just simply cause a great deal of problems: these people are like walking problems spreading problems anywhere they can. These people are not easy to avoid and some act deliberately so that they can screw up your life perfectly and so don't do what you desire. We can prevent the harm they cause through the use of this magick.

Magick with Baal for victory over problem people

(You will need a length of rope long enough to tie several knots in and wide enough in girth for those very same knots to be easy to untie)

Leviathan you are a great monster a powerful devil and your mouth is the very mouth of Hell itself; the Hell Mouth. Leviathan I ask that you open your mouth that which is the gateway of Hell itself; the Gates of Hell. Leviathan open the gates open your mouth: Leviathan opens its mouth the Gates of Hell are open.

TIE THE FIRST KNOT IN THE ROPE

I summon the demonic entity known as Baal through the Gates of Hell. Baal first King of Hell I ask that you step through the gateway and be right here with me: Baal steps through the gates and is here with me.

TIE A SECOND KNOT IN THE ROPE

Baal you are the first King of Hell, he with three heads, one of a toad, one of a man and one of a cat and you have 66 legions of demons at your control. Baal, I ask that you make me victorious over all problem people and this is what I ask of you.

TIE A THIRD KNOT

Baal agrees and departs back through the gates. Leviathan you are a great monster a powerful devil and your mouth is the very mouth of Hell itself; the Hell Mouth. Leviathan I ask that you shut your mouth that which is the gateway of Hell itself; the Gates of Hell.

Leviathan close the gates close your mouth: Leviathan closes its mouth the Gates of Hell are shut.

TIE A FOURTH KNOT

So it is and will be.

You have expanded your concept of this rope magick and have some knowledge of Baal. The truth is that what is here is here to assist you so your life will be made better. I feel that in life we have opportunities which boost us or drag us down. I wish you to go up and achieve greater things: but maybe this is because this is what I myself dream of: of achieving more: I have already written over 480 books almost all on occultism: real magick: which is more than anyone has ever written in all of history, but more would be nice. But what you wish in your life is for you to choose and my success may not be yours. I know that tom speculate is one thing and yet this book is based also on the solid nature of rope. In fact it is easy

18

to forget that in this book one of the greatest heroes of this magick is the length of rope you use yourself to work magick. When you think of it the power of magick is perhaps less important than the simply knowing it exists because when we add this into our mental box: the brain: much of life starts to make sense and we can easily grasp that a lot of what we think of as being the complete picture isn't and we understand that much is hidden from view and knowing this we can reconstruct what occurs in situations we otherwise would have no solution for.

Chapter 3

Asmodai is a king of Hell with three heads one of a bull, one of a man and one of a ram. Asmodai even has the power to spurt forth flames from it's mouth. This next magick therefore connects with the latter of these traits well, because it is fire that we will be using. However never forget that Asmodai still has two legions of spirits at its command. For this next magick however you will need to have some person you know quite well and wish to do great harm to: if not then perhaps pick a dictator to practice on: will what follows to work and it shall.

Magick with Asmodai to burn a chosen person

(You will need a length of rope long enough to tie several knots in and wide enough in girth for those very same knots to be easy to untie)

20

Leviathan you are a great monster a powerful devil and your mouth is the very mouth of Hell itself; the Hell Mouth. Leviathan I ask that you open your mouth that which is the gateway of Hell itself; the Gates of Hell. Leviathan open the gates open your mouth: Leviathan opens its mouth the Gates of Hell are open.

TIE THE FIRST KNOT IN THE ROPE

I summon the demonic entity known as Asmodai through the Gates of Hell. Asmodai King of Hell I ask that you step through the gateway and be right here with me: Asmodai steps through the gates and is here with me.

TIE A SECOND KNOT IN THE ROPE

Asmodai you are a King of Hell, he with three heads, one of a bull, one of a man and one of a ram and a serpentine tail and from your mouth flames may spurt forth and you have two legions of spirits at your control. Asmodai, I ask that you burn <u>state name of chosen person</u> and this is what I ask of you.

TIE A THIRD KNOT

Asmodai agrees and departs back through the gates. Leviathan you are a great monster a powerful devil and your mouth is the very mouth of Hell itself; the Hell Mouth. Leviathan I ask that you shut your mouth that which is the gateway of Hell itself; the Gates of Hell. Leviathan close the gates close your mouth: Leviathan closes its mouth the Gates of Hell are shut.

TIE A FOURTH KNOT

So it is and will be.

This following magick is to burn a location and so you should have some location in mind that is your target. You should already be familiar with the location or use maps and pictures: these can easily be found usually on the internet: to familiarize yourself with the location. Once done you may then work magick to burn it if you desire.

Magick with Asmodai to burn a chosen location

(You will need a length of rope long enough to tie several knots in and wide enough in girth for those very same knots to be easy to untie)

Leviathan you are a great monster a powerful devil and your mouth is the very mouth of Hell itself; the Hell Mouth. Leviathan I ask that you open your mouth that which is the gateway of Hell itself; the Gates of Hell. Leviathan open the gates open your mouth: Leviathan opens its mouth the Gates of Hell are open.

TIE THE FIRST KNOT IN THE ROPE

I summon the demonic entity known as Asmodai through the Gates of Hell. Asmodai King of Hell I ask that you step through the gateway and be right here with me: Asmodai steps through the gates and is here with me.

TIE A SECOND KNOT IN THE ROPE

Asmodai you are a King of Hell, he with three heads, one of a bull, one of a man and one of a ram and a serpentine tail and from your mouth flames may spurt forth and you have two legions of spirits at your control. Asmodai, I ask that you burn state name of chosen location and this is what I ask of you.

TIE A THIRD KNOT

Asmodai agrees and departs back through the gates. Leviathan you are a great monster a powerful devil and your mouth is the very mouth of Hell itself; the Hell Mouth. Leviathan I ask that you shut your mouth that which is the gateway of Hell itself; the Gates of Hell. Leviathan close the gates close your mouth: Leviathan closes its mouth the Gates of Hell are shut.

TIE A FOURTH KNOT

So it is and will be.

Organizations generally have people that make it up: all companies and organizations have members or employees of some sort. This magick will attack the people that are of that organization. However, the problem with this is it will not pick out the good people and leave these alone but if this is what you desire then there is no problem: this magick follows.

Magick with Asmodai to burn the people of a chosen organization

(You will need a length of rope long enough to tie several knots in and wide enough in girth for those very same knots to be easy to untie)

Leviathan you are a great monster a powerful devil and your mouth is the very mouth of Hell itself; the Hell Mouth. Leviathan I ask

that you open your mouth that which is the gateway of Hell itself;

the Gates of Hell. Leviathan open the gates open your mouth:

Leviathan opens its mouth the Gates of Hell are open.

TIE THE FIRST KNOT IN THE ROPE

I summon the demonic entity known as Asmodai through the Gates

of Hell. Asmodai King of Hell I ask that you step through the

gateway and be right here with me: Asmodai steps through the

gates and is here with me.

TIE A SECOND KNOT IN THE ROPE

Asmodai you are a King of Hell, he with three heads, one of a bull,

one of a man and one of a ram and a serpentine tail and from your

mouth flames may spurt forth and you have two legions of spirits at

your control. Asmodai, I ask that you burn all the people within the

organization named <u>state name of chosen organization</u> and this is

what I ask of you.

26

TIE A THIRD KNOT

Asmodai agrees and departs back through the gates. Leviathan you are a great monster a powerful devil and your mouth is the very mouth of Hell itself; the Hell Mouth. Leviathan I ask that you shut your mouth that which is the gateway of Hell itself; the Gates of Hell. Leviathan close the gates close your mouth: Leviathan closes its mouth the Gates of Hell are shut.

TIE A FOURTH KNOT

So it is and will be.

Each and every one of us has enemies even if we are unaware of them. This following magick will burn your enemies even if you do not know who they are. In fact, this magick therefore helps you to keep safe because a dead or injured enemy is less of a threat than one intact. I will now tell you how to work this magick.

Magick with Asmodai to burn all enemies

(You will need a length of rope long enough to tie several knots in and wide enough in girth for those very same knots to be easy to untie)

Leviathan you are a great monster a powerful devil and your mouth is the very mouth of Hell itself; the Hell Mouth. Leviathan I ask that you open your mouth that which is the gateway of Hell itself; the Gates of Hell. Leviathan open the gates open your mouth: Leviathan opens its mouth the Gates of Hell are open.

TIE THE FIRST KNOT IN THE ROPE

I summon the demonic entity known as Asmodai through the Gates of Hell. Asmodai King of Hell I ask that you step through the gateway and be right here with me: Asmodai steps through the gates and is here with me.

TIE A SECOND KNOT IN THE ROPE

Asmodai you are a King of Hell, he with three heads, one of a bull, one of a man and one of a ram and a serpentine tail and from your mouth flames may spurt forth and you have two legions of spirits at your control. Asmodai, I ask that you burn all my enemies and this is what I ask of you.

TIE A THIRD KNOT

Asmodai agrees and departs back through the gates. Leviathan you are a great monster a powerful devil and your mouth is the very mouth of Hell itself; the Hell Mouth. Leviathan I ask that you shut your mouth that which is the gateway of Hell itself; the Gates of Hell. Leviathan close the gates close your mouth: Leviathan closes its mouth the Gates of Hell are shut.

TIE A FOURTH KNOT

So it is and will be.

You have now some knowledge and hopefully some experience of the devil named Asmodai. In this way therefore you are growing and yet still exactly the same person that you were when you started this book.

Chapter 4

The magick in this chapter is protective and so the first is to protect you: this seems a sensible way to start; I actually advise that you use this magick because it is difficult to be overprotected. But for this following magick to work and keep working you must will it to work as you perform the ritual and keep the knots tied in the rope: labelling the rope is also a good idea.

Magick with Asmodai to protect you

(You will need a length of rope long enough to tie several knots in and wide enough in girth for those very same knots to be easy to untie)

Leviathan you are a great monster a powerful devil and your mouth is the very mouth of Hell itself; the Hell Mouth. Leviathan I ask that you open your mouth that which is the gateway of Hell itself;

the Gates of Hell. Leviathan open the gates open your mouth: Leviathan opens its mouth the Gates of Hell are open.

TIE THE FIRST KNOT IN THE ROPE

I summon the demonic entity known as Asmodai through the Gates of Hell. Asmodai King of Hell I ask that you step through the gateway and be right here with me: Asmodai steps through the gates and is here with me.

TIE A SECOND KNOT IN THE ROPE

Asmodai you are a King of Hell, he with three heads, one of a bull, one of a man and one of a ram and a serpentine tail and from your mouth flames may spurt forth and you have two legions of spirits at your control. Asmodai, I ask that you protect me from all harm and all attacks and this is what I ask of you.

TIE A THIRD KNOT

Asmodai agrees and departs back through the gates. Leviathan you are a great monster a powerful devil and your mouth is the very mouth of Hell itself; the Hell Mouth. Leviathan I ask that you shut your mouth that which is the gateway of Hell itself; the Gates of Hell. Leviathan close the gates close your mouth: Leviathan closes its mouth the Gates of Hell are shut.

TIE A FOURTH KNOT

So it is and will be.

I feel it is a good idea to protect our friends because obviously why not help those you find you wish to spend life or time with. Plus, when friends are in trouble sometimes, we get sucked in and so our life is easier if those close to us are protected.

Magick with Asmodai to protect your friends

(You will need a length of rope long enough to tie several knots in and wide enough in girth for those very same knots to be easy to untie)

Leviathan you are a great monster a powerful devil and your mouth is the very mouth of Hell itself; the Hell Mouth. Leviathan I ask that you open your mouth that which is the gateway of Hell itself; the Gates of Hell. Leviathan open the gates open your mouth: Leviathan opens its mouth the Gates of Hell are open.

TIE THE FIRST KNOT IN THE ROPE

I summon the demonic entity known as Asmodai through the Gates of Hell. Asmodai King of Hell I ask that you step through the gateway and be right here with me: Asmodai steps through the gates and is here with me.

TIE A SECOND KNOT IN THE ROPE

Asmodai you are a King of Hell, he with three heads, one of a bull, one of a man and one of a ram and a serpentine tail and from your mouth flames may spurt forth and you have two legions of spirits at your control. Asmodai, I ask that you protect my friends from all harm and all attacks and this is what I ask of you.

TIE A THIRD KNOT

Asmodai agrees and departs back through the gates. Leviathan you are a great monster a powerful devil and your mouth is the very mouth of Hell itself; the Hell Mouth. Leviathan I ask that you shut your mouth that which is the gateway of Hell itself; the Gates of Hell. Leviathan close the gates close your mouth: Leviathan closes its mouth the Gates of Hell are shut.

TIE A FOURTH KNOT

So it is and will be.

For the same reason we may choose to protect our friends we also may wish to protect our family. But do remember with this magick simply by untying the knots you can undo any of the magick in this book: yes, it really is that simple. Will what follows to work and it shall.

Magick with Asmodai to protect your family

(You will need a length of rope long enough to tie several knots in and wide enough in girth for those very same knots to be easy to untie)

Leviathan you are a great monster a powerful devil and your mouth is the very mouth of Hell itself; the Hell Mouth. Leviathan I ask that you open your mouth that which is the gateway of Hell itself; the Gates of Hell. Leviathan open the gates open your mouth: Leviathan opens its mouth the Gates of Hell are open.

TIE THE FIRST KNOT IN THE ROPE

I summon the demonic entity known as Asmodai through the Gates of Hell. Asmodai King of Hell I ask that you step through the gateway and be right here with me: Asmodai steps through the gates and is here with me.

TIE A SECOND KNOT IN THE ROPE

Asmodai you are a King of Hell, he with three heads, one of a bull, one of a man and one of a ram and a serpentine tail and from your mouth flames may spurt forth and you have 2 legions of spirits at your control. Asmodai, I ask that you protect my family from all harm and all attacks and this is what I ask of you.

TIE A THIRD KNOT

Asmodai agrees and departs back through the gates. Leviathan you are a great monster a powerful devil and your mouth is the very mouth of Hell itself; the Hell Mouth. Leviathan I ask that you shut your mouth that which is the gateway of Hell itself; the Gates of

Hell. Leviathan close the gates close your mouth: Leviathan closes its mouth the Gates of Hell are shut.

TIE A FOURTH KNOT

So it is and will be.

With this magick you will be able tom protect anyone of your choosing. However, it is best if it is someone you are familiar with: know well enough to know their name and what they look like. This next magick is potent and here it is.

Magick with Asmodai to protect someone of your choosing

(You will need a length of rope long enough to tie several knots in and wide enough in girth for those very same knots to be easy to untie)

Leviathan you are a great monster a powerful devil and your mouth is the very mouth of Hell itself; the Hell Mouth. Leviathan I ask that you open your mouth that which is the gateway of Hell itself;

38

the Gates of Hell. Leviathan open the gates open your mouth: Leviathan opens its mouth the Gates of Hell are open.

TIE THE FIRST KNOT IN THE ROPE

I summon the demonic entity known as Asmodai through the Gates of Hell. Asmodai King of Hell I ask that you step through the gateway and be right here with me: Asmodai steps through the gates and is here with me.

TIE A SECOND KNOT IN THE ROPE

Asmodai you are a King of Hell, he with three heads, one of a bull, one of a man and one of a ram and a serpentine tail and from your mouth flames may spurt forth and you have two legions of spirits at your control. Asmodai, I ask that you protect state name of chosen person from all harm and all attacks and this is what I ask of you.

TIE A THIRD KNOT

Asmodai agrees and departs back through the gates. Leviathan you are a great monster a powerful devil and your mouth is the very mouth of Hell itself; the Hell Mouth. Leviathan I ask that you shut your mouth that which is the gateway of Hell itself; the Gates of Hell. Leviathan close the gates close your mouth: Leviathan closes its mouth the Gates of Hell are shut.

TIE A FOURTH KNOT

So it is and will be.

You have gained in knowledge, power and perhaps even wisdom because if magick such as this can work for you it means that other people can work it against you or for themselves. But never think that because these demonic beings are potent that you are not central because obviously you are crucial and yet they do add strength and power.

Chapter 5

I will be teaching you now how to summon and work rope magick with a devil named Beleth. Beleth is a demonic being that controls eighty-five legions of demons. Beleth also rides a war horse and so is linked to war and violence as all kings of Hell are. The next magick is rope magick to disembowel someone of your choosing; and the rope element means that it shall keep attacking the person unless you untie the knots. Will what follows to work and it shall.

Magick with Beleth to disembowel a chosen person

(You will need a length of rope long enough to tie several knots in and wide enough in girth for those very same knots to be easy to untie)

Leviathan you are a great monster a powerful devil and your mouth is the very mouth of Hell itself; the Hell Mouth. Leviathan I ask that you open your mouth that which is the gateway of Hell itself;

the Gates of Hell. Leviathan open the gates open your mouth: Leviathan opens its mouth the Gates of Hell are open.

TIE THE FIRST KNOT IN THE ROPE

I summon the demonic entity known as Beleth through the Gates of Hell. Beleth King of Hell I ask that you step through the gateway and be right here with me: Beleth steps through the gates and is here with me.

TIE A SECOND KNOT IN THE ROPE

Beleth you are a King of Hell who rides a war horse and as you travel music follows, Beleth the mighty he who controls eighty-five legions of demons. Beleth, I ask that you disembowel state name of chosen person and this is what I ask of you.

TIE A THIRD KNOT

Beleth agrees and departs back through the gates. Leviathan you are a great monster a powerful devil and your mouth is the very mouth of Hell itself; the Hell Mouth. Leviathan I ask that you shut your mouth that which is the gateway of Hell itself; the Gates of Hell. Leviathan close the gates close your mouth: Leviathan closes its mouth the Gates of Hell are shut.

TIE A FOURTH KNOT

So it is and will be.

Our eyes are important and as the wearer of spectacles I understand this. I think it is the case that if you work this magick not just can you affect someone's eyesight but you can untie the knots and make their eyes normal. In fact, do this repeatedly: casting spells undoing them will disorient them a lot.

Magick with Beleth to attack the eyesight of a chosen person

(You will need a length of rope long enough to tie several knots in and wide enough in girth for those very same knots to be easy to untie)

Leviathan you are a great monster a powerful devil and your mouth is the very mouth of Hell itself; the Hell Mouth. Leviathan I ask that you open your mouth that which is the gateway of Hell itself; the Gates of Hell. Leviathan open the gates open your mouth: Leviathan opens its mouth the Gates of Hell are open.

TIE THE FIRST KNOT IN THE ROPE

I summon the demonic entity known as Beleth through the Gates of Hell. Beleth King of Hell I ask that you step through the gateway and be right here with me: Beleth steps through the gates and is here with me.

TIE A SECOND KNOT IN THE ROPE

Beleth you are a King of Hell who rides a war horse and as you travel music follows, Beleth the mighty he who controls eighty-five legions of demons. Beleth, I ask that you attack the eyesight of state name of chosen person and this is what I ask of you.

44

TIE A THIRD KNOT

Beleth agrees and departs back through the gates. Leviathan you are a great monster a powerful devil and your mouth is the very mouth of Hell itself; the Hell Mouth. Leviathan I ask that you shut your mouth that which is the gateway of Hell itself; the Gates of Hell. Leviathan close the gates close your mouth: Leviathan closes its mouth the Gates of Hell are shut.

TIE A FOURTH KNOT

So it is and will be.

You will now learn how to target your magick to a target so it will get cut. Yes, that's right you will be getting this magick to cut someone of your choosing. However, you must still desire strongly this magick to work as you perform the following ritual.

Magick with Beleth to cut a chosen person

(You will need a length of rope long enough to tie several knots in and wide enough in girth for those very same knots to be easy to untie)

Leviathan you are a great monster a powerful devil and your mouth is the very mouth of Hell itself; the Hell Mouth. Leviathan I ask that you open your mouth that which is the gateway of Hell itself; the Gates of Hell. Leviathan open the gates open your mouth: Leviathan opens its mouth the Gates of Hell are open.

TIE THE FIRST KNOT IN THE ROPE

I summon the demonic entity known as Beleth through the Gates of Hell. Beleth King of Hell I ask that you step through the gateway and be right here with me: Beleth steps through the gates and is here with me.

TIE A SECOND KNOT IN THE ROPE

46

Beleth you are a King of Hell who rides a war horse and as you travel music follows, Beleth the mighty he who controls eighty-five legions of demons. Beleth, I ask that you cut state name of chosen person again and again forever more and this is what I ask of you.

TIE A THIRD KNOT

Beleth agrees and departs back through the gates. Leviathan you are a great monster a powerful devil and your mouth is the very mouth of Hell itself; the Hell Mouth. Leviathan I ask that you shut your mouth that which is the gateway of Hell itself; the Gates of Hell. Leviathan close the gates close your mouth: Leviathan closes its mouth the Gates of Hell are shut.

TIE A FOURTH KNOT

So it is and will be.

This following magick will cause anyone at a location of your choosing to get cut. This will keep happening until you untie the

47

knots on the rope that sustain the magick: the magick keeps working until you untie the knots on the rope.

Magick with Beleth to cut everyone at a chosen location

(You will need a length of rope long enough to tie several knots in and wide enough in girth for those very same knots to be easy to untie)

Leviathan you are a great monster a powerful devil and your mouth is the very mouth of Hell itself; the Hell Mouth. Leviathan I ask that you open your mouth that which is the gateway of Hell itself; the Gates of Hell. Leviathan open the gates open your mouth: Leviathan opens its mouth the Gates of Hell are open.

TIE THE FIRST KNOT IN THE ROPE

I summon the demonic entity known as Beleth through the Gates of Hell. Beleth King of Hell I ask that you step through the gateway and be right here with me: Beleth steps through the gates and is here with me.

TIE A SECOND KNOT IN THE ROPE

Beleth you are a King of Hell who rides a war horse and as you travel music follows, Beleth the mighty he who controls eighty-five legions of demons. Beleth, I ask that you cut everyone at <u>state address or chosen location</u> cut them forever more and this is what I ask of you.

TIE A THIRD KNOT

Beleth agrees and departs back through the gates. Leviathan you are a great monster a powerful devil and your mouth is the very mouth of Hell itself; the Hell Mouth. Leviathan I ask that you shut your mouth that which is the gateway of Hell itself; the Gates of Hell. Leviathan close the gates close your mouth: Leviathan closes its mouth the Gates of Hell are shut.

TIE A FOURTH KNOT

So it is and will be.

The strength of your magick has increased. I feel this is as it should be because as you progress you learn more even grow in experience and so from this flows power. It means that you have more choice than you have probably had at any point in your life: you cannot choose whether to work magick you do not know. A powerful person cannot be made into a slave: and if you were a slave you have probably freed yourself: I wish to free all the slaves.

Chapter 6

The magic in this chapter is devoted to that most fantastic of things victory. However, in order to be victorious: to possess victory: we need something or someone to be victorious over. But the world being an imperfect place this is usually not too difficult: problems exist to be overcome. This magick works and here it is.

Magick with Beleth to be victorious over all problems

(You will need a length of rope long enough to tie several knots in and wide enough in girth for those very same knots to be easy to untie)

Leviathan you are a great monster a powerful devil and your mouth is the very mouth of Hell itself; the Hell Mouth. Leviathan I ask that you open your mouth that which is the gateway of Hell itself; the Gates of Hell. Leviathan open the gates open your mouth: Leviathan opens its mouth the Gates of Hell are open.

TIE THE FIRST KNOT IN THE ROPE

I summon the demonic entity known as Beleth through the Gates of Hell. Beleth King of Hell I ask that you step through the gateway and be right here with me: Beleth steps through the gates and is here with me.

TIE A SECOND KNOT IN THE ROPE

Beleth you are a King of Hell who rides a war horse and as you travel music follows, Beleth the mighty he who controls eighty-five legions of demons. Beleth, I ask that you to make me victorious over all problems and this is what I ask of you.

TIE A THIRD KNOT

Beleth agrees and departs back through the gates. Leviathan you are a great monster a powerful devil and your mouth is the very mouth of Hell itself; the Hell Mouth. Leviathan I ask that you shut your mouth that which is the gateway of Hell itself; the Gates of

52

Hell. Leviathan close the gates close your mouth: Leviathan closes its mouth the Gates of Hell are shut.

TIE A FOURTH KNOT

So it is and will be.

This following magick in some ways could be thought of as protective even because it attacks attackers, although this does mean they attacked you first whereas most protective magick would protect you from being attacked. But this is good magick to use alongside protective magick; and here it is.

Magick with Beleth to be victorious over any attackers

(You will need a length of rope long enough to tie several knots in and wide enough in girth for those very same knots to be easy to untie)

Leviathan you are a great monster a powerful devil and your mouth is the very mouth of Hell itself; the Hell Mouth. Leviathan I ask

that you open your mouth that which is the gateway of Hell itself; the Gates of Hell. Leviathan open the gates open your mouth: Leviathan opens its mouth the Gates of Hell are open.

TIE THE FIRST KNOT IN THE ROPE

I summon the demonic entity known as Beleth through the Gates of Hell. Beleth King of Hell I ask that you step through the gateway and be right here with me: Beleth steps through the gates and is here with me.

TIE A SECOND KNOT IN THE ROPE

Beleth you are a King of Hell who rides a war horse and as you travel music follows, Beleth the mighty he who controls eighty-five legions of demons. Beleth, I ask that you to make me victorious over any attackers and this is what I ask of you.

TIE A THIRD KNOT

Beleth agrees and departs back through the gates. Leviathan you are a great monster a powerful devil and your mouth is the very mouth of Hell itself; the Hell Mouth. Leviathan I ask that you shut your mouth that which is the gateway of Hell itself; the Gates of Hell. Leviathan close the gates close your mouth: Leviathan closes its mouth the Gates of Hell are shut.

TIE A FOURTH KNOT

So it is and will be.

Violent situations happen whether we want them to or not it takes only one to create violence and yet the attacker is not necessarily victorious. But my aim is to make sure that you are victorious whether you are the attacker or not and I do this with this following magick.

Magick with Beleth to be victorious in violent situations

(You will need a length of rope long enough to tie several knots in and wide enough in girth for those very same knots to be easy to untie)

Leviathan you are a great monster a powerful devil and your mouth is the very mouth of Hell itself; the Hell Mouth. Leviathan I ask that you open your mouth that which is the gateway of Hell itself; the Gates of Hell. Leviathan open the gates open your mouth: Leviathan opens its mouth the Gates of Hell are open.

TIE THE FIRST KNOT IN THE ROPE

I summon the demonic entity known as Beleth through the Gates of Hell. Beleth King of Hell I ask that you step through the gateway and be right here with me: Beleth steps through the gates and is here with me.

TIE A SECOND KNOT IN THE ROPE

Beleth you are a King of Hell who rides a war horse and as you travel music follows, Beleth the mighty he who controls eighty-five legions of demons. Beleth, I ask that you to make me victorious in any violent situation and this is what I ask of you.

TIE A THIRD KNOT

Beleth agrees and departs back through the gates. Leviathan you are a great monster a powerful devil and your mouth is the very mouth of Hell itself; the Hell Mouth. Leviathan I ask that you shut your mouth that which is the gateway of Hell itself; the Gates of Hell. Leviathan close the gates close your mouth: Leviathan closes its mouth the Gates of Hell are shut.

TIE A FOURTH KNOT

So it is and will be.

We all have enemies it seems and so I will show you how to work this potent magick. I understand that the thoughts of enemies and dealing with them makes some people feel uncomfortable and yet I feel personally that this magick here is quite necessary. But as always, the choice is yours: in fact, I would have it no other way.

Magick with Beleth to be victorious over all enemies

(You will need a length of rope long enough to tie several knots in and wide enough in girth for those very same knots to be easy to untie)

Leviathan you are a great monster a powerful devil and your mouth is the very mouth of Hell itself; the Hell Mouth. Leviathan I ask that you open your mouth that which is the gateway of Hell itself; the Gates of Hell. Leviathan open the gates open your mouth: Leviathan opens its mouth the Gates of Hell are open.

TIE THE FIRST KNOT IN THE ROPE

I summon the demonic entity known as Beleth through the Gates of Hell. Beleth King of Hell I ask that you step through the gateway and be right here with me: Beleth steps through the gates and is here with me.

TIE A SECOND KNOT IN THE ROPE

Beleth you are a King of Hell who rides a war horse and as you travel music follows, Beleth the mighty he who controls eighty-five legions of demons. Beleth, I ask that you to make me victorious over all enemies and this is what I ask of you.

TIE A THIRD KNOT

Beleth agrees and departs back through the gates. Leviathan you are a great monster a powerful devil and your mouth is the very mouth of Hell itself; the Hell Mouth. Leviathan I ask that you shut your mouth that which is the gateway of Hell itself; the Gates of Hell. Leviathan close the gates close your mouth: Leviathan closes its mouth the Gates of Hell are shut.

TIE A FOURTH KNOT

So it is and will be.

I know that my now you have come to understand the power even a simply item such as a rope can have. The fact is that life is a potent thing and it can assist us in many ways. I feel that we should embrace the opportunities and new knowledge that life has set out for us. I know as well as anyone that life isn't all it seems to be and that often situations do not look to be what they are on the surface. But this is how adventures happen and yes how people get hurt. If we are thinking we are in less trouble than we otherwise would be. I feel it is the one who can react quickly when needed and work out which way they must go and what to do that survives things. To survive is wonderful and if you keep doing it endlessly you are immortal.

Chapter 7

The demon Bathin has power over travel and it is said that he may take you anywhere in a moment: to travel in no time at all. I therefore first show you magick to make your enemies lost when around you so they are unable to act against you: will this magick to work and it shall, keep the knots tied and it will keep on working.

Magick with Bathin to make it so that all your enemies get lost when around you

(You will need a length of rope long enough to tie several knots in and wide enough in girth for those very same knots to be easy to untie)

Leviathan you are a great monster a powerful devil and your mouth is the very mouth of Hell itself; the Hell Mouth. Leviathan I ask that you open your mouth that which is the gateway of Hell itself;

the Gates of Hell. Leviathan open the gates open your mouth: Leviathan opens its mouth the Gates of Hell are open.

TIE THE FIRST KNOT IN THE ROPE

I summon the demonic entity known as Bathin through the Gates of Hell. Bathin Duke of Hell I ask that you step through the gateway and be right here with me: Bathin steps through the gates and is here with me.

TIE A SECOND KNOT IN THE ROPE

Bathin you are a Duke of Hell, you are strong and ride a pale horse, Bathin the mighty he who commands thirty legions of demons, Bathin the strong man with a snake's tail and riding a pale horse. Bathin, I ask that you to make all my enemies be lost when around me this is what I ask of you.

TIE A THIRD KNOT

Bathin agrees and departs back through the gates. Leviathan you are a great monster a powerful devil and your mouth is the very mouth of Hell itself; the Hell Mouth. Leviathan I ask that you shut your mouth that which is the gateway of Hell itself; the Gates of Hell. Leviathan close the gates close your mouth: Leviathan closes its mouth the Gates of Hell are shut.

TIE A FOURTH KNOT

So it is and will be.

This next magick will take and effectively trap someone of your choosing at a location of your choosing. The person should ideally be someone you know well enough to know what they look like and their name and the location should be one you are either familiar with or one you have looked at on maps and on any pictures or video you can get of the area.

Magick with Bathin for a chosen person to be at a chosen location

(You will need a length of rope long enough to tie several knots in and wide enough in girth for those very same knots to be easy to untie)

Leviathan you are a great monster a powerful devil and your mouth is the very mouth of Hell itself; the Hell Mouth. Leviathan I ask that you open your mouth that which is the gateway of Hell itself; the Gates of Hell. Leviathan open the gates open your mouth: Leviathan opens its mouth the Gates of Hell are open.

TIE THE FIRST KNOT IN THE ROPE

I summon the demonic entity known as Bathin through the Gates of Hell. Bathin Duke of Hell I ask that you step through the gateway and be right here with me: Bathin steps through the gates and is here with me.

TIE A SECOND KNOT IN THE ROPE

Bathin you are a Duke of Hell you are strong and ride a pale horse,
Bathin the mighty he who commands thirty legions of demons,
Bathin the strong man with a snake's tail and riding a pale horse.
Bathin, I ask that you take <u>state name of chosen person</u> to <u>state</u>
<u>chosen address or location</u> and this is what I ask of you.

TIE A THIRD KNOT

Bathin agrees and departs back through the gates. Leviathan you
are a great monster a powerful devil and your mouth is the very
mouth of Hell itself; the Hell Mouth. Leviathan I ask that you shut
your mouth that which is the gateway of Hell itself; the Gates of
Hell. Leviathan close the gates close your mouth: Leviathan closes
its mouth the Gates of Hell are shut.

TIE A FOURTH KNOT

So it is and will be.

In life we sometimes get lost and this is more than an inconvenience because it may cost us our lives or property depending on where exactly we are lost in. The truth is that dangerous places are everywhere and we are best to avoid them: unless we live there in which case this is impossible. The truth is that we are now expanding the types of rope magick you learn and can do. We need some variation when we work this magick because we never know what our requirements will be.

Magick with Bathin to always get where you want to go

(You will need a length of rope long enough to tie several knots in and wide enough in girth for those very same knots to be easy to untie)

Leviathan you are a great monster a powerful devil and your mouth is the very mouth of Hell itself; the Hell Mouth. Leviathan I ask that you open your mouth that which is the gateway of Hell itself;

the Gates of Hell. Leviathan open the gates open your mouth: Leviathan opens its mouth the Gates of Hell are open.

TIE THE FIRST KNOT IN THE ROPE

I summon the demonic entity known as Bathin through the Gates of Hell. Bathin Duke of Hell I ask that you step through the gateway and be right here with me: Bathin steps through the gates and is here with me.

TIE A SECOND KNOT IN THE ROPE

Bathin you are a Duke of Hell you are strong and ride a pale horse, Bathin the mighty he who commands thirty legions of demons, Bathin the strong man with a snake's tail and riding a pale horse. Bathin, I ask that you to make it so that I always make it to where I want to go and this is what I ask of you.

TIE A THIRD KNOT

Bathin agrees and departs back through the gates. Leviathan you are a great monster a powerful devil and your mouth is the very mouth of Hell itself; the Hell Mouth. Leviathan I ask that you shut your mouth that which is the gateway of Hell itself; the Gates of Hell. Leviathan close the gates close your mouth: Leviathan closes its mouth the Gates of Hell are shut.

TIE A FOURTH KNOT

So it is and will be.

It is easy to be hurt when travelling because we are out of our environment and even the best of us can get things stolen, or attacked. This is because the criminal is in their best position|: a familiar location: whereas you are not. In fact, they probably already have a plan and help and you are likely to have neither of these things.

Magick with Bathin for protection when travelling

(You will need a length of rope long enough to tie several knots in and wide enough in girth for those very same knots to be easy to untie)

Leviathan you are a great monster a powerful devil and your mouth is the very mouth of Hell itself; the Hell Mouth. Leviathan I ask that you open your mouth that which is the gateway of Hell itself; the Gates of Hell. Leviathan open the gates open your mouth: Leviathan opens its mouth the Gates of Hell are open.

TIE THE FIRST KNOT IN THE ROPE

I summon the demonic entity known as Bathin through the Gates of Hell. Bathin Duke of Hell I ask that you step through the gateway and be right here with me: Bathin steps through the gates and is here with me.

TIE A SECOND KNOT IN THE ROPE

Bathin you are a Duke of Hell you are strong and ride a pale horse,

Bathin the mighty he who commands thirty legions of demons,

Bathin the strong man with a snake's tail and riding a pale horse.

Bathin, I ask that you protect me when travelling and this is what I

ask of you.

TIE A THIRD KNOT

Bathin agrees and departs back through the gates. Leviathan you

are a great monster a powerful devil and your mouth is the very

mouth of Hell itself; the Hell Mouth. Leviathan I ask that you shut

your mouth that which is the gateway of Hell itself; the Gates of

Hell. Leviathan close the gates close your mouth: Leviathan closes

its mouth the Gates of Hell are shut.

TIE A FOURTH KNOT

So it is and will be.

You have now been introduced to Bathin and he surely is a worthwhile and practical entity to use for magick. I know that for many the advantages of magick do not seem a draw to them and yet it offers so much for us all. Do as you desire however although I recommend that you finish the last and desirable chapter.

Chapter 8

We all of us can find ourselves in a fight because often it doesn't take two to choose it takes just one because once, we are attacked instinct comes in and we fight or sometimes not just get hurt but may even die. This is the reason why I offer this next magick to win fights. Keep the knots tied in the rope and it will work as a talisman and will help to keep you winning.

Magick with Bathin to win fights

(You will need a length of rope long enough to tie several knots in and wide enough in girth for those very same knots to be easy to untie)

Leviathan you are a great monster a powerful devil and your mouth is the very mouth of Hell itself; the Hell Mouth. Leviathan I ask that you open your mouth that which is the gateway of Hell itself;

the Gates of Hell. Leviathan open the gates open your mouth: Leviathan opens its mouth the Gates of Hell are open.

TIE THE FIRST KNOT IN THE ROPE

I summon the demonic entity known as Bathin through the Gates of Hell. Bathin Duke of Hell I ask that you step through the gateway and be right here with me: Bathin steps through the gates and is here with me.

TIE A SECOND KNOT IN THE ROPE

Bathin you are a Duke of Hell you are strong and ride a pale horse, Bathin the mighty he who commands thirty legions of demons, Bathin the strong man with a snake's tail and riding a pale horse. Bathin, I ask that you help me to win any fights this is what I ask of you.

TIE A THIRD KNOT

Bathin agrees and departs back through the gates. Leviathan you are a great monster a powerful devil and your mouth is the very mouth of Hell itself; the Hell Mouth. Leviathan I ask that you shut your mouth that which is the gateway of Hell itself; the Gates of Hell. Leviathan close the gates close your mouth: Leviathan closes its mouth the Gates of Hell are shut.

TIE A FOURTH KNOT

So it is and will be.

I think that difficulties often teach us something because we do the same thing unless we are forced to change: this is the habit of many people. Difficulties and problems exist to be overcome that is life we may not have a magick bomb all the time: or do we: but we do have a small knife or hammer and we just slash or chip away and doing this we eventually win. Get help overcoming all difficulties like this.

Magick with Bathin overcome all difficulties

(You will need a length of rope long enough to tie several knots in and wide enough in girth for those very same knots to be easy to untie)

Leviathan you are a great monster a powerful devil and your mouth is the very mouth of Hell itself; the Hell Mouth. Leviathan I ask that you open your mouth that which is the gateway of Hell itself; the Gates of Hell. Leviathan open the gates open your mouth: Leviathan opens its mouth the Gates of Hell are open.

TIE THE FIRST KNOT IN THE ROPE

I summon the demonic entity known as Bathin through the Gates of Hell. Bathin Duke of Hell I ask that you step through the gateway and be right here with me: Bathin steps through the gates and is here with me.

TIE A SECOND KNOT IN THE ROPE

Bathin you are a Duke of Hell you are strong and ride a pale horse, Bathin the mighty he who commands thirty legions of demons, Bathin the strong man with a snake's tail and riding a pale horse. Bathin, I ask that you to help me overcome all difficulties and this is what I ask of you.

TIE A THIRD KNOT

Bathin agrees and departs back through the gates. Leviathan you are a great monster a powerful devil and your mouth is the very mouth of Hell itself; the Hell Mouth. Leviathan I ask that you shut your mouth that which is the gateway of Hell itself; the Gates of Hell. Leviathan close the gates close your mouth: Leviathan closes its mouth the Gates of Hell are shut.

TIE A FOURTH KNOT

So it is and will be.

Bathin does have the ability to attack via his thirty legions of demons. I know that at times we must attack and yet I know this is something many other people do not approve of. I will be honest I can see the advantages personally in the monks existence and the way they are not violent: such as Buddhist and Christian monks but I don't think I would wish others to die because of them, because we our selves may choose death if we desire it but I feel the problem would remain and it may cause the death of another because dying is far easier than living.

Magick with Bathin to attack a chosen person

(You will need a length of rope long enough to tie several knots in and wide enough in girth for those very same knots to be easy to untie)

Leviathan you are a great monster a powerful devil and your mouth is the very mouth of Hell itself; the Hell Mouth. Leviathan I ask

that you open your mouth that which is the gateway of Hell itself; the Gates of Hell. Leviathan open the gates open your mouth: Leviathan opens its mouth the Gates of Hell are open.

TIE THE FIRST KNOT IN THE ROPE

I summon the demonic entity known as Bathin through the Gates of Hell. Bathin Duke of Hell I ask that you step through the gateway and be right here with me: Bathin steps through the gates and is here with me.

TIE A SECOND KNOT IN THE ROPE

Bathin you are a Duke of Hell you are strong and ride a pale horse, Bathin the mighty he who commands thirty legions of demons, Bathin the strong man with a snake's tail and riding a pale horse. Bathin, I ask that you and your legions attack state name of chosen person and this is what I ask of you.

TIE A THIRD KNOT

Bathin agrees and departs back through the gates. Leviathan you are a great monster a powerful devil and your mouth is the very mouth of Hell itself; the Hell Mouth. Leviathan I ask that you shut your mouth that which is the gateway of Hell itself; the Gates of Hell. Leviathan close the gates close your mouth: Leviathan closes its mouth the Gates of Hell are shut.

TIE A FOURTH KNOT

So it is and will be.

Sometimes what we must attack isn't a person but an organization. However, in order to attack an organization, we will find that partly we attack those working for and within the organization itself. However, sabotage is also useful and yet I am asking you through this magick to leave the exact details to Bathin so that he can attack the organization you wish to be attacked for you.

Magick with Bathin to attack a chosen organization

(You will need a length of rope long enough to tie several knots in and wide enough in girth for those very same knots to be easy to untie)

Leviathan you are a great monster a powerful devil and your mouth is the very mouth of Hell itself; the Hell Mouth. Leviathan I ask that you open your mouth that which is the gateway of Hell itself; the Gates of Hell. Leviathan open the gates open your mouth: Leviathan opens its mouth the Gates of Hell are open.

TIE THE FIRST KNOT IN THE ROPE

I summon the demonic entity known as Bathin through the Gates of Hell. Bathin Duke of Hell I ask that you step through the gateway and be right here with me: Bathin steps through the gates and is here with me.

TIE A SECOND KNOT IN THE ROPE

Bathin you are a Duke of Hell you are strong and ride a pale horse,

Bathin the mighty he who commands thirty legions of demons,

Bathin the strong man with a snake's tail and riding a pale horse.

Bathin, I ask that you attack the organization known as state name

of organization and this is what I ask of you.

TIE A THIRD KNOT

Bathin agrees and departs back through the gates. Leviathan you

are a great monster a powerful devil and your mouth is the very

mouth of Hell itself; the Hell Mouth. Leviathan I ask that you shut

your mouth that which is the gateway of Hell itself; the Gates of

Hell. Leviathan close the gates close your mouth: Leviathan closes

its mouth the Gates of Hell are shut.

TIE A FOURTH KNOT

So it is and will be.

You have now come to the end of this book and yet there is still more you can learn if you wish and as the author of over 480 books almost all on occultism, I hope you may consider reading more of these. However, in life there is always more to learn and sometimes more important more to do because it is through our actions and thoughts that we change ourselves and the world for the better.

www.ingramcontent.com/pod-product-compliance
Lightning Source LLC
La Vergne TN
LVHW021542080426
835509LV00019B/2783